WIT AND WISDOM

EDITED BY DAVID PLAUT

RUNNING PRESS

PHILADELPHIA, PENNSYLVANIA

A Running Press Miniature Edition™
Copyright © 1992 by Running Press. Printed in
Singapore/Hong Kong. All rights reserved under the Pan-
American and International Copyright Conventions.

This book may not be reproduced in whole or in part in any
form or by any means, electronic or mechanical, including
photocopying, recording, or by any information storage and
retrieval system now known or hereafter invented, without
written permission from the publisher.
The proprietary trade dress, including the size and format of
this Running Press Miniature Edition™, is the property of
Running Press. It may not be used or reproduced without the
express written permission of Running Press.

Canadian representatives: General Publishing Co., Ltd., 30
Lesmill Road, Don Mills, Ontario M3B 2T6.
International representatives: Worldwide Media Services, Inc.,
115 East Twenty-third Street, New York, NY 10010.

9 8 7 6 5 4 3 2 1
Digit on the right indicates the number of this printing.

Library of Congress
Cataloging-in-publication Number 91–50911
ISBN 1–56138–104–7

This book may be ordered from the publisher. Please add
$1.00 postage and handling. *But try your bookstore first!*
Running Press Book Publishers
125 South Twenty-second Street
Philadelphia, Pennsylvania 19103

INTRODUCTION

Why is baseball so compelling? The attraction begins early, when parents teach their children to play catch in the backyard. Gradually, kids move onto Little League, high school, and American Legion ball. The talented young men play in college, and, if lucky, then sign with the pros and head to the minors, hoping some day to make it to "The Show"—the major leagues. The rest of us chart their progress, living vicariously through their triumphs and failures, while still lustily swinging our bats in neighborhood parks on the Fourth of July. A first love is not easily forgotten.

Baseball is a common experience, part of America's collective past. Many observers respect its rhythms of cause and effect, victory and defeat, hero and goat. Some fans simply relax within its leisurely tempo. Baseball becomes a safe and familiar haven from the accelerating pace of a world that seems to grow more uncertain each day.

In attempts to understand baseball's grip on the nation, many of our greatest writers have offered explanation through words of poetic elegance. Ballplayers have their own unique opinions about the national pastime. Their sage, sarcastic, witty, and ironic comments could only come from those who have lived the complexities of the game.

Here then is a collection of quotes on the enduring appeal of baseball, offered by presidents, pitchers, scholars, and second basemen. They span more than one hundred years of the baseball experience, holding a mirror to the grand old game so that we can better appreciate it— and in so doing gain a greater understanding of ourselves.

In the beginning, there was no baseball. But ever since there have been few beginnings as good as the start of a new baseball season. It is the most splendid time in sport.

B. J. Phillips
Time (1981)

. . . THE DIAMONDS AND THE RITUALS
OF BASEBALL CREATE AN ELEGANT,
TRIVIAL, ENCHANTED GRID ON WHICH
OUR SUFFERING SHAPELESS SINFUL DAY
LEANS FOR THE MOMENTARY GRACE OF
ORDER.

DONALD HALL
"BASEBALL AND THE
MEANING OF LIFE" (1985)

WHOEVER WANTS TO KNOW THE HEART

AND MIND OF AMERICA HAD BETTER

LEARN BASEBALL.

JACQUES BARZUN
"GOD'S COUNTRY AND MINE" (1954)

I SEE GREAT THINGS IN BASEBALL. IT'S OUR GAME—THE AMERICAN GAME. IT WILL TAKE OUR PEOPLE OUT OF DOORS, FILL THEM WITH OXYGEN, GIVE THEM A LARGER PHYSICAL STOICISM. TEND TO RELIEVE US FROM BEING A NERVOUS, DYSPEPTIC SET. REPAIR THESE LOSSES, AND BE A BLESSING TO US.

WALT WHITMAN (1819–1892)
POET

I THINK A BASEBALL FIELD MUST BE THE MOST BEAUTIFUL THING IN THE WORLD. IT'S SO HONEST AND PRECISE. AND WE PLAY ON IT. EVERY STAR GETS HUMBLED. EVERY MEDIOCRE PLAYER HAS A GREAT MOMENT.

LOWELL COHN
"THE TEMPLE OF BASEBALL" (1981)

NINETY FEET BETWEEN THE BASES IS

THE NEAREST THING TO PERFECTION

THAT MAN HAS YET ACHIEVED.

RED SMITH (1905–1982)
SPORTSWRITER

Any baseball is beautiful. No other small package comes as close to the ideal in design and utility. It is a perfect object for a man's hand. Pick it up and it instantly suggests its purpose: it is meant to be thrown a considerable distance— thrown hard and with precision.

ROGER ANGELL
FIVE SEASONS (1977)

MAN MAY PENETRATE THE OUTER REACHES OF THE UNIVERSE. HE MAY SOLVE THE VERY SECRET OF ETERNITY ITSELF BUT FOR ME, THE ULTIMATE HUMAN EXPERIENCE IS TO WITNESS THE FLAWLESS EXECUTION OF THE HIT-AND-RUN.

BRANCH RICKEY
DODGERS GENERAL MANAGER (1943–50)

Honus Wagner

THE CLOCK DOESN'T MATTER IN BASE-
BALL. TIME STANDS STILL OR MOVES
BACKWARD. THEORETICALLY, ONE GAME
COULD GO ON FOREVER. SOME SEEM TO.

HERB CAEN
SAN FRANCISCO CHRONICLE (1979)

I BELIEVE IN THE RIP VAN WINKLE THEORY—THAT A MAN FROM 1910 MUST BE ABLE TO WAKE UP AFTER BEING ASLEEP FOR SEVENTY YEARS, WALK INTO A BALL-PARK AND UNDERSTAND BASEBALL PER-FECTLY.

BOWIE KUHN
COMMISSIONER OF BASEBALL (1969–84)

OREL HERSHISER

BASEBALL IS THE ONLY THING BE-
SIDES THE PAPER CLIP THAT HASN'T
CHANGED.

BILL VEECK
INDIANS OWNER (1946-50)

No game in the world is as tidy and dramatically neat as baseball, with cause and effect, crime and punishment, motive and result, so cleanly defined.

PAUL GALLICO (1897–1976)
SPORTSWRITER

BASEBALL TO ME IS STILL THE NATION-
AL PASTIME BECAUSE IT IS A SUMMER
GAME. I FEEL THAT ALMOST ALL AMERI-
CANS ARE SUMMER PEOPLE, THAT SUM-
MER IS WHAT THEY THINK OF WHEN THEY
THINK OF THEIR CHILDHOOD. I THINK IT
STIRS UP AN INCREDIBLE EMOTION WI-
THIN PEOPLE.

STEVE BUSBY
ROYALS PITCHER (1972–80)

BOYS WOULD BE BIG LEAGUERS, AS
EVERYBODY KNOWS, BUT SO WOULD BIG
LEAGUERS BE BOYS.

PHILIP ROTH
THE GREAT AMERICAN NOVEL (1973)

You gotta be a man to play baseball for a living, but you gotta have a lot of little boy in you.

ROY CAMPANELLA
DODGERS CATCHER (1948–57)

When I was a small boy in Kansas, a friend of mine and I went fishing. . . . I told him I wanted to be a real major league baseball player, a genuine professional like Honus Wagner. My friend said that he'd like to be President of the United States. Neither of us got our wish.

Dwight D. Eisenhower
(1890–1969)
34th President of the United States

GROWING UP IS A RITUAL—MORE DEADLY THAN RELIGION, MORE COMPLICATED THAN BASEBALL, FOR THERE SEEMED TO BE NO RULES. EVERYTHING IS EXPERIENCED FOR THE FIRST TIME. BUT BASEBALL CAN SOOTHE EVEN THOSE PAINS, FOR IT IS STABLE AND PERMANENT, STEADY AS A GRANDFATHER DOZING IN A WICKER CHAIR ON A VERANDAH.

W.P. KINSELLA
SHOELESS JOE (1982)

. . .I FEEL AN INVISIBLE BOND BE-
TWEEN OUR THREE GENERATIONS, AN
ANCHOR OF LOYALTY LINKING MY SONS
TO THE GRANDFATHER WHOSE FACE
THEY NEVER SAW BUT WHOSE PERSON
THEY HAVE ALREADY COME TO KNOW
THROUGH THIS MOST TIMELESS OF ALL
SPORTS, THE GAME OF BASEBALL.

DORIS KEARNS GOODWIN
"FROM FATHER WITH LOVE" (1987)

BASEBALL FOR SEVEN INNINGS ONLY IS LIKE DINNER WITHOUT COGNAC AT THE END. IT IS LIKE KISSING THE WOMAN YOU LOVE GOODNIGHT BY BLOWING IT FROM YOUR FINGERS.

ROBERT FONTAINE
"THE HAPPY TIME" (1946)

LOU GEHRIG

THE STRONGEST THING BASEBALL HAS

GOING FOR IT TODAY IS YESTERDAYS.

LAWRENCE RITTER
THE GLORY OF THEIR TIMES (1966)

BASEBALL IS REALLY TWO SPORTS—THE SUMMER GAME AND THE AUTUMN GAME. ONE IS THE LEISURELY PASTIME OF OUR NATIONAL MYTHOLOGY. THE OTHER IS NOT SO GENTLE.

THOMAS BOSWELL
HOW LIFE IMITATES THE WORLD SERIES (1982)

BASEBALL IS A GAME, YES. IT IS ALSO A BUSINESS. BUT WHAT IT MOST TRULY IS IS DISGUISED COMBAT. FOR ALL ITS GENTILITY, ITS ALMOST LEISURELY PACE, BASEBALL IS VIOLENCE UNDER WRAPS.

WILLIE MAYS
GIANTS OUTFIELDER (1951–73)

THE GREAT AMERICAN GAME SHOULD BE

AN UNRELENTING WAR OF NERVES.

TY COBB
TIGERS OUTFIELDER (1905—26)

TY COBB

THE GREAT THING ABOUT BASEBALL IS
THAT THERE'S A CRISIS EVERY DAY.

GABE PAUL
YANKEES PRESIDENT (1973–77)

LOVE AMERICA AND HATE BASEBALL?

HATE AMERICA AND LOVE BASEBALL?

NEITHER IS POSSIBLE, EXCEPT IN THE

ABSTRACT.

JOHN KRICH
EL BEISBOL (1989)

It is the sport that a foreigner is least likely to take to. You have to grow up playing it, you have to accept the lore of the bubble gum card, and believe that if the answer to the Mays-Mantle-Snider question is found, then the universe will be a simpler and more ordered place.

DAVID HALBERSTAM, B. 1934
AUTHOR

THERE HAVE BEEN ONLY TWO GENIUSES IN THE WORLD. WILLIE MAYS AND WILLIE SHAKESPEARE.

TALLULAH BANKHEAD (1903–1968)
ACTRESS

WILLIE MAYS

Baseball reflected the language of America, and spiced it, too. Presidents, politicians, executives, generals and parents touched all the bases regularly so that nobody would be out in left field or caught off base in the greater pursuits of life. If you did it right, you hit a grand slam home run; if not, you struck out.

Joseph Durso
Baseball and the American Dream (1986)

THE BEST BASEBALL PEOPLE ARE CAR-
TESIANS. THAT IS, THEY APPLY DES-
CARTES' METHODS TO THEIR CRAFT,
BREAKING IT DOWN INTO BITE-SIZE COM-
PONENTS, MASTERING THEM AND THEN
BUILDING THE CRAFT UP, BIT BY
BIT. . . . MASTER ENOUGH LITTLE
PROBLEMS AND YOU WILL HAVE FEW BIG
PROBLEMS.

GEORGE WILL
MEN AT WORK (1990)

HANK AARON

BASEBALL IS DEMOCRACY IN ACTION: IN IT ALL MEN ARE "FREE AND EQUAL," REGARDLESS OF RACE, NATIONALITY, OR CREED. EVERY MAN IS GIVEN THE RIGHTFUL OPPORTUNITY TO RISE TO THE TOP ON HIS OWN MERITS.... IT IS THE FULLEST EXPRESSION OF FREEDOM OF SPEECH, FREEDOM OF PRESS, AND FREEDOM OF ASSEMBLY IN OUR NATIONAL LIFE.

FRANCIS TREVELYAN MILLER
INTRODUCTION TO CONNIE MACK'S
MY SIXTY-SIX YEARS IN BASEBALL (1950)

HUMANITY IS THE KEYSTONE THAT HOLDS NATIONS AND MEN TOGETHER. WHEN THAT COLLAPSES, THE WHOLE STRUCTURE CRUMBLES. THIS IS AS TRUE OF BASEBALL TEAMS AS ANY OTHER PURSUIT IN LIFE.

CONNIE MACK
ATHLETICS MANAGER (1901–50)

EVERY DAY IS A NEW OPPORTUNITY. YOU CAN BUILD ON YESTERDAY'S SUCCESS OR PUT ITS FAILURES BEHIND AND START OVER AGAIN. THAT'S THE WAY LIFE IS, WITH A NEW GAME EVERY DAY, AND THAT'S THE WAY BASEBALL IS.

BOB FELLER
INDIANS PITCHER (1936–56)

ONE OF THE BEAUTIFUL THINGS ABOUT

BASEBALL IS THAT EVERY ONCE IN A

WHILE YOU COME INTO A SITUATION

WHERE YOU WANT TO, AND WHERE YOU

HAVE TO, REACH DOWN AND PROVE

SOMETHING.

NOLAN RYAN
METS/ANGELS/ASTROS/
RANGERS PITCHER (1966–)

NOLAN RYAN

I'D WALK THROUGH HELL IN A GASOLINE

SUIT TO KEEP PLAYING BASEBALL.

PETE ROSE
REDS/PHILLIES/EXPOS
INFIELDER (1963—86)

BASEBALL GIVES YOU EVERY CHANCE TO BE GREAT. THEN IT PUTS PRESSURE ON YOU TO PROVE THAT YOU HAVEN'T GOT WHAT IT TAKES. IT NEVER TAKES AWAY THE CHANCE, AND IT NEVER EASES UP ON THE PRESSURE.

JOE GARAGIOLA
BASEBALL IS A FUNNY GAME (1960)

SATCHEL PAIGE

I AIN'T EVER HAD A JOB. I JUST ALWAYS

PLAYED BASEBALL.

LEROY ROBERT "SATCHEL" PAIGE
NEGRO LEAGUES/INDIANS/BROWNS
PITCHER (1926–53, 1965)

I LOVED THE GAME. I LOVED THE COMPE-

TITION. BUT I NEVER HAD ANY FUN. I

NEVER ENJOYED IT. ALL HARD WORK, ALL

THE TIME.

CARL YASTRZEMSKI
RED SOX OUTFIELDER (1961–83)

1961
ROOKIE

CARL YASTRZEMSKI
Outfield

Boston
Red Sox

It's tomorrow that counts. So you worry all the time. It never ends. Lord, baseball is a worrying thing.

STANLEY COVELESKI
INDIANS PITCHER (1916–24)

CASEY STENGEL

GEORGE BRETT

No one can stop a home run. No one can understand what it really is, unless you have felt it in your own hands and body. . . . As the ball makes its high, long arc beyond the playing field, the diamond and the stands suddenly belong to one man. In that brief, brief time, you are free of all demands and complications.

SADAHARU OH
TOKYO GIANTS OUTFIELDER (1959–80)

How hard is hitting? You ever walk into a pitch-black room full of furniture that you've never been in before and try to walk through it without bumping into anything? Well, it's harder than that.

TED KLUSZEWSKI
REDS FIRST BASEMAN (1947–57)

THE GREATEST THRILL IN THE WORLD
IS TO END THE GAME WITH A HOME RUN
AND WATCH EVERYBODY ELSE WALK
OFF THE FIELD WHILE YOU'RE RUNNING
THE BASES ON AIR.

AL ROSEN
INDIANS THIRD BASEMAN (1947–56)

BASEBALL IS THE ONLY FIELD OF EN-
DEAVOR WHERE A MAN CAN SUCCEED
THREE TIMES OUT OF TEN AND BE CON-
SIDERED A GOOD PERFORMER.

TED WILLIAMS
RED SOX OUTFIELDER (1939–60)

TED WILLIAMS

outfield **BOSTON RED SOX**

Ted Williams

THEY'LL KEEP YOU IN THERE GENER'LY,
AS LONG AS YOU CAN HIT. IF YOU CAN
SMACK THAT OLE APPLE, THEY'LL SEND
YOU OUT THERE IF THEY'VE GOT TO USE
GLUE TO KEEP YOU FROM FALLIN' APART.

THOMAS WOLFE
YOU CAN'T GO HOME AGAIN (1940)

WHEN YOU'RE IN A SLUMP, IT'S ALMOST
AS IF YOU LOOK OUT AT THE FIELD AND
IT'S ONE BIG GLOVE.

VANCE LAW
PIRATES/WHITE SOX/EXPOS/
CUBS/A'S INFIELDER (1980–)

BASEBALL IS A GAME WHERE A CURVE
IS AN OPTICAL ILLUSION. A SCREWBALL
CAN BE A PITCH OR A PERSON, STEAL-
ING IS LEGAL AND YOU CAN SPIT ANY-
WHERE YOU LIKE EXCEPT IN THE
UMPIRE'S EYE OR ON THE BALL.

JIM MURRAY
LOS ANGELES TIMES (1962)

UMPIRE'S HEAVEN IS A PLACE WHERE HE
WORKS THIRD BASE EVERY GAME. HOME
IS WHERE THE HEARTACHE IS.

RON LUCIANO
AMERICAN LEAGUE UMPIRE (1968–80)

LET'S FACE IT. UMPIRING IS NOT AN EASY OR HAPPY WAY TO MAKE A LIVING. IN THE ABUSE THEY SUFFER, AND THE PAY THEY GET FOR IT, YOU SEE AN IMBALANCE THAT CAN ONLY BE EXPLAINED BY THEIR NEED TO STAY CLOSE TO A GAME THEY CAN'T RESIST.

BOB UECKER
CATCHER IN THE WRY (1982)

The game has a cleanness. If you do a good job, the numbers say so. You don't have to ask anyone or play politics. You don't have to wait for the reviews.

SANDY KOUFAX
DODGERS PITCHER (1955–66)

SANDY KOUFAX

NOTHING FLATTERS ME MORE THAN TO HAVE IT ASSUMED THAT I COULD WRITE PROSE—UNLESS IT BE TO HAVE IT ASSUMED THAT I ONCE PITCHED A BASEBALL WITH DISTINCTION.

ROBERT FROST (1874–1963)
POET

THE PITCHER IS HAPPIEST WITH HIS ARM IDLE. HE PREFERS TO DAWDLE IN THE PRESENT, KNOWING THAT AS SOON AS HE GETS ON THE MOUND AND STARTS HIS WINDUP, HE DELIVERS HIMSELF TO THE UNCERTAINTY OF THE FUTURE.

GEORGE PLIMPTON
Out of My League (1961)

LEO DUROCHER

YOU DON'T SAVE A PITCHER FOR TOMOR-

ROW. TOMORROW IT MAY RAIN.

> LEO DUROCHER
> DODGERS/GIANTS/CUBS/ASTROS
> MANAGER (1939–55, 1966–73)

It's no fun throwing fastballs to guys who can't hit them. The real challenge is getting them out on stuff they can hit.

SAM McDOWELL
Indians pitcher (1961–71)

ROGER CLEMENS

OH, HELL, IF YOU WIN TWENTY GAMES

THEY WANT YOU TO DO IT EVERY YEAR.

BILLY LOES
DODGERS/ORIOLES/GIANTS
PITCHER (1950–61)

THE TWO MOST IMPORTANT THINGS IN
LIFE ARE GOOD FRIENDS AND A STRONG
BULLPEN.

BOB LEMON
ROYALS/WHITE SOX/YANKEES
MANAGER (1970–72, 1977–79, 1981–82)

THERE ARE ONLY TWO PLACES IN THIS
LEAGUE. FIRST PLACE AND NO PLACE.

TOM SEAVER
METS/REDS/WHITE SOX
PITCHER (1967–83)

IF A TIE IS LIKE KISSING YOUR SISTER,

LOSING IS LIKE KISSING YOUR GRAND-

MOTHER WITH HER TEETH OUT.

GEORGE BRETT
ROYALS INFIELDER (1973–)

SPARKY ANDERSON

THERE SHOULD BE A NEW WAY TO RE-
CORD STANDINGS IN THIS LEAGUE: ONE
COLUMN FOR WINS, ONE FOR LOSSES
AND ONE FOR GIFTS.

GENE MAUCH
PHILLIES MANAGER (1960–68)

BASEBALL IS LIKE CHURCH. MANY
ATTEND, BUT FEW UNDERSTAND.

WES WESTRUM
METS MANAGER (1965–67)

JACKIE ROBINSON

BASEBALL IS LIKE A POKER GAME. NO-
BODY WANTS TO QUIT WHEN HE'S
LOSING; NOBODY WANTS YOU TO QUIT
WHEN YOU'RE AHEAD.

JACKIE ROBINSON
DODGERS INFIELDER (1947–56)

BASEBALL IS A LOT LIKE LIFE. THE LINE DRIVES ARE CAUGHT, THE SQUIBBERS GO FOR BASE HITS. IT'S AN UNFAIR GAME.

ROD KANEHL
METS INFIELDER (1962–64)

ANY TIME YOU THINK YOU HAVE THE GAME CONQUERED, THE GAME WILL TURN AROUND AND PUNCH YOU RIGHT IN THE NOSE.

MIKE SCHMIDT
PHILLIES THIRD BASEMAN (1972–88)

When we lost I couldn't sleep at night. When we win I can't sleep at night. But when you win, you wake up feeling better.

JOE TORRE
METS/BRAVES/CARDINALS
MANAGER (1977–84 1990–)

THE ONLY WAY TO PROVE YOU'RE A GOOD

SPORT IS TO LOSE.

ERNIE BANKS
CUBS INFIELDER (1953–71)

I CANNOT GET RID OF THE HURT FROM LOSING . . . . BUT AFTER THE LAST OUT OF EVERY LOSS, I MUST ACCEPT THAT THERE'LL BE A TOMORROW. IN FACT, IT'S MORE THAN THERE'LL BE A TOMORROW: IT'S THAT I WANT THERE TO BE A TOMORROW. THAT'S THE BIG DIFFERENCE. I WANT TOMORROW TO COME.

SPARKY ANDERSON
REDS/TIGERS MANAGER (1970–)

BASEBALL IS THE BEST SPORT FOR A
WRITER TO COVER, BECAUSE IT'S DAILY.
IT'S ONGOING. YOU HAVE TO FILL THE
NEED, WRITE THE DAILY SOAP OPERA.

PETER GAMMONS
BOSTON GLOBE (1978)

If you've ever been around a group of actors, you've noticed, no doubt, that they can talk of nothing else under the sun but acting . . . It's exactly the same way with baseball players. Your heart must be in your work.

CHRISTY MATHEWSON
GIANTS PITCHER (1900–16)

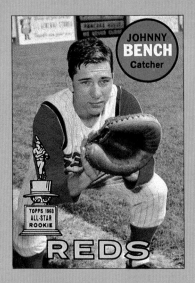

It is the best of all games for me.
It frequently escapes from the pattern of sport and assumes the form of a virile ballet. . . . The movement is natural and unrehearsed and controlled only by the unexpected flight of the ball.

JIMMY CANNON (1910–1973)
SPORTSWRITER

LAST YEAR, MORE AMERICANS WENT TO SYMPHONIES THAN WENT TO BASEBALL GAMES. THIS MAY BE VIEWED AS AN ALARMING STATISTIC, BUT I THINK THAT BOTH BASEBALL AND THE COUNTRY WILL ENDURE.

JOHN F. KENNEDY (1917–63)
35TH PRESIDENT OF THE
UNITED STATES

THERE ARE TWO CLASSES OF PEOPLE
WHOSE WEALTH IS ALWAYS EXAGGERAT-
ED BY THE GREAT PUBLIC. THEY ARE
ACTORS AND BALLPLAYERS.

MIKE "KING" KELLY
WHITE SOX CATCHER (1880–86)

A BALLPLAYER HAS TWO REPUTATIONS, ONE WITH THE OTHER PLAYERS AND ONE WITH THE FANS. THE FIRST IS BASED ON ABILITY. THE SECOND THE NEWSPAPERS GIVE HIM.

JOHNNY EVERS
CUBS INFIELDER (1902–13)

DARRYL STRAWBERRY

REGGIE JACKSON

FANS DON'T BOO NOBODIES.

REGGIE JACKSON
A'S/ORIOLES/YANKEES/ANGELS
OUTFIELDER (1967—87)

A GUY WHO'S PLAYED ONE GAME IN THE

PROS IS LIKE A FORMER STATE SENATOR,

A BIG MAN IN MOST NEIGHBORHOODS

AND ANY SALOON AS LONG AS HE LIVES.

WILFRID SHEED
"DIAMONDS ARE FOREVER" (1985)

A BASEBALL CLUB IS PART OF THE CHEMISTRY OF THE CITY. A GAME ISN'T JUST AN ATHLETIC CONTEST. IT'S A PICNIC, A KIND OF TOWN MEETING.

MICHAEL BURKE
YANKEES PRESIDENT (1967–73)

WHILE YOU'RE PLAYING BALL, YOU'RE IN-
SULATED. ALL THE BALLPARKS AND THE
BIG CROWDS HAVE A CERTAIN MYSTIQUE.
YOU FEEL ATTACHED, PERMANENTLY
WEDDED TO THE SOUNDS THAT RING OUT,
TO THE FANS CHANTING YOUR NAME,
EVEN WHEN THERE ARE ONLY FOUR OR
FIVE THOUSAND IN THE STANDS ON A
WEDNESDAY AFTERNOON.

MICKEY MANTLE
YANKEES OUTFIELDER (1951–68)

MICKEY MANTLE

outfielder NEW YORK YANKEES

THE GUY WITH THE BIGGEST STOMACH

WILL BE THE FIRST TO TAKE OFF HIS

SHIRT AT A BASEBALL GAME.

GLENN DICKEY
SAN FRANCISCO CHRONICLE (1981)

IF PEOPLE DON'T WANT TO COME TO THE
BALLPARK, HOW ARE YOU GONNA STOP
THEM?

YOGI BERRA
YANKEES/METS MANAGER
(1964 1972−75, 1984−85)

YOGI BERRA

WITH THOSE WHO DON'T GIVE A DAMN ABOUT BASEBALL, I CAN ONLY SYMPATHIZE. I DO NOT RESENT THEM. I AM EVEN WILLING TO CONCEDE THAT MANY OF THEM ARE PHYSICALLY CLEAN, GOOD TO THEIR MOTHERS AND IN FAVOR OF WORLD PEACE. BUT WHILE THE GAME IS ON, I CAN'T THINK OF ANYTHING TO SAY TO THEM.

ART HILL
I DON'T CARE IF I NEVER COME BACK (1980)

THE MAJORITY OF AMERICAN MALES PUT
THEMSELVES TO SLEEP BY STRIKING OUT
THE BATTING ORDER OF THE NEW YORK
YANKEES.

JAMES THURBER (1894–1961)
WRITER

A BASEBALL FAN HAS THE DIGESTIVE AP-
PARATUS OF A BILLY GOAT. HE CAN, AND
DOES, DEVOUR ANY SET OF DIAMOND
STATISTICS WITH AN INSATIABLE APPE-
TITE AND THEN NUZZLES HUNGRILY FOR
MORE.

ARTHUR DALEY (1904–1974)
SPORTSWRITER

TELL A BALLPLAYER SOMETHING A THOUSAND TIMES, THEN TELL HIM AGAIN, BECAUSE THAT MIGHT BE THE TIME HE'LL UNDERSTAND SOMETHING.

PAUL RICHARDS
WHITE SOX/ORIOLES
MANAGER (1951–61, 1976)

THE MANAGER'S TOUGHEST JOB IS NOT
CALLING THE RIGHT PLAY WITH THE
BASES FULL AND THE SCORE TIED IN AN
EXTRA INNING GAME. IT'S TELLING A
BALLPLAYER THAT HE'S THROUGH, DONE,
FINISHED.

JIMMIE DYKES
WHITE SOX MANAGER (1934–46)

You start chasing a ball and your brain immediately commands your body to "Run forward! Bend! Scoop up the ball! Peg it to the infield!" Then your body says "Who, me?"

JOE DiMAGGIO
YANKEES OUTFIELDER (1936–51)

JOE DiMaggio

I'M THROWING TWICE AS HARD AS I EVER

DID. IT'S JUST NOT GETTING THERE AS

FAST.

LEFTY GOMEZ
YANKEES PITCHER (1930–43)

IT'S A MERE MOMENT IN A MAN'S LIFE
BETWEEN THE ALL-STAR GAME AND AN
OLD-TIMER'S GAME.

VIN SCULLY, B. 1927
DODGERS BROADCASTER

BABE RUTH

ALL BALLPLAYERS SHOULD QUIT WHEN
IT STARTS TO FEEL AS IF ALL THE BASE-
LINES RUN UPHILL.

BABE RUTH
YANKEES OUTFIELDER (1920–34)

He missed the sensation of the sock—the moment the stomach galloped just before the wood hit the ball, and the satisfying sting that sped through his arms and shoulders as he belted one . . . He missed the special exercise of running the bases, whirling 'round them with the speed of a racehorse as nine frantic men tried to cut him down.

BERNARD MALAMUD
THE NATURAL (1952)

I WOULD BE LOST WITHOUT BASEBALL. I

DON'T THINK I COULD STAND BEING

AWAY FROM IT AS LONG AS I WAS ALIVE.

ROBERTO CLEMENTE
PIRATES OUTFIELDER (1955–1972)

I THINK YOU MUST LOOK INWARD BECAUSE "INSIDE" IS WHERE IT'S COMING FROM: OTHERWISE, WHAT WOULD THE GAME MEAN BUT TIN SOLDIERS ON A TOY FIELD, OR DATA POURING THROUGH COMPUTER TERMINALS? . . . . THROUGHOUT THOSE EXTRA INNINGS, I KEPT ASKING MYSELF— WHY? WHY DOES THIS (WHICH MEANS NOTHING AT ALL) MEAN SO MUCH I CAN BARELY BREATHE?

RICHARD GROSSINGER
"THE DREAM LIFE OF JOHNNY BASEBALL (1987)

INN SCORE

AND SO, FINALLY, HE FOUND HIS WAY
BACK TO BASEBALL. NOTHING LIKE IT,
REALLY. . . . NO OTHER ACTIVITY IN THE
WORLD HAD SO PRECISE AND COMPRE-
HENSIVE A HISTORY, SO SPECIFIC AN
EPIC, AND AT THE SAME TIME, STRANGE
AS IT SEEMED, SO MUCH ULTIMATE
MYSTERY.

ROBERT COOVER
THE UNIVERSAL BASEBALL ASSOCIATION (1968)

It is designed to break your heart. The game begins in the spring, when everything else begins again, and it blossoms in the summer, filling the afternoons and evenings, and then as soon as the chill rains come, it stops and leaves you to face the fall alone.

A. Bartlett Giamatti
Commissioner of Baseball, 1989
"The Green Fields of the Mind" (1975)

You spend a good piece of your life gripping a baseball and in the end it turns out that it was the other way around all the time.

JIM BOUTON
BALL FOUR (1970)

Look for these favorite
Running Press Miniature Editions™

Aesop's Fables

The Artistic Cat

As a Man Thinketh

Audubon's Birds

Baseball Wit and Wisdom

A Christmas Carol

Edward Lear's Nonsense ABCs

Emily Dickinson: Selected Poems

Friendship: A Bouquet of Quotes

The Language of Flowers

The Literary Cat

The Little Book of Christmas Carols

The Little Book of Hand Shadows

Love: Quotations from the Heart

Love Sonnets of Shakespeare

Motherhood

The Night Before Christmas

Quotable Women

The Miniature Mother Goose

Tales from the Arabian Nights

Tales of Peter Rabbit

The Velveteen Rabbit

The Wit and Wisdom of Mark Twain

Women's Wit and Wisdom

This book has been bound using handcraft methods, and Smythe-sewn to ensure durability.
The dust jacket was designed by Toby Schmidt
The interior was designed by Christian Benton
The photographs were researched by Gillian Speeth.
The front and back dust jacket illustrations are by Michael A. Schacht.
Additional front jacket illustration by Christian Benton.
Photo credits: pages 3, 116 © 1990 L.O.L. Inc., FPG International Corporation; page 7 Rick Stewart/Allsport USA; pages 9, 135 D. Strohmeyer/Allsport USA; pages 12, 86, 110 © 1988 Richard Mackson, FPG International Corporation; page 16, © 1989 Cezus, FPG International Corporation; pages 19, 80 Culver

Pictures; page 22 Don Smith/Allsport USA; page 27 Scott Halleran/Allsport USA; page 31 Jansen/H. Armstrong Roberts; pages 34, 41, 50, 58, 61, 69, 103, 115, 130 courtesy National Baseball Library, Cooperstown, N.Y.; pages 37, 38, 70, 83, 89, 95, 106, and endpapers Otto Greule Jr./Allsport USA; page 44 J.D. Cuban/Allsport USA; page 47 UPI/Bettman Newsphotos; page 55 © 1991 Zimmerman, FPG International Corporation; pages 63, 77 FPG International Corporation; page 64 Jonathan Daniel/Allsport USA; pages 92, 119, 127 AP/Wide World Photos; page 98 Nathan Bilow/Allsport USA; page 109 Stephen Dunn/Allsport USA; page 124 Kirk Schlea/Allsport USA; page 136 Robert Beck/Allsport USA.

The text was set in Copperplate, with ITC Franklin Gothic, by Commcor Communications Corporation, Philadelphia, Pennsylvania.

BASEBALL

WIT AND

WISDOM